ERIC CHAKEEN

And Away They Go

Del Mar, CA has a population of 4,161. My drivers license still counts me as one of them. The Del Mar Racetrack situated in this small town holds 44,000. This massive stadium, built for excess and consumption, long loomed over my life there and the magnetism of this beautiful and debauched place felt like the town orbited around this fading sun. The popularity of horse racing in Del Mar is waning.

I have gone back every holiday, every break from work, attempting to suss out what makes this place of extreme highs and vacuous lows so attractive. The track's ocean view provides a ready-made allegory for the track's activity, the way bettors ride crests of momentum, even achieving temporary flight, before crashing, mimicking the cyclical tides lapping at its shores. The palms and sunscreen mix with the smell of spent adrenaline and stale beer, making a singular bouquet evocative of my youth.

The entire range of human experience exists in the two minutes after the horses leave the starting gates. The expenditure and subsequent come-down leaves a jarring, melancholic aftertaste in contrast to the pastoral surroundings.

I find a certain solace stalking around this monolith to old Hollywood, spying on patrons both close at heart and far from mind.

California Chrome

DEL MAR
cool as ever
Phone
5
10
25
50¢

DEL MAR

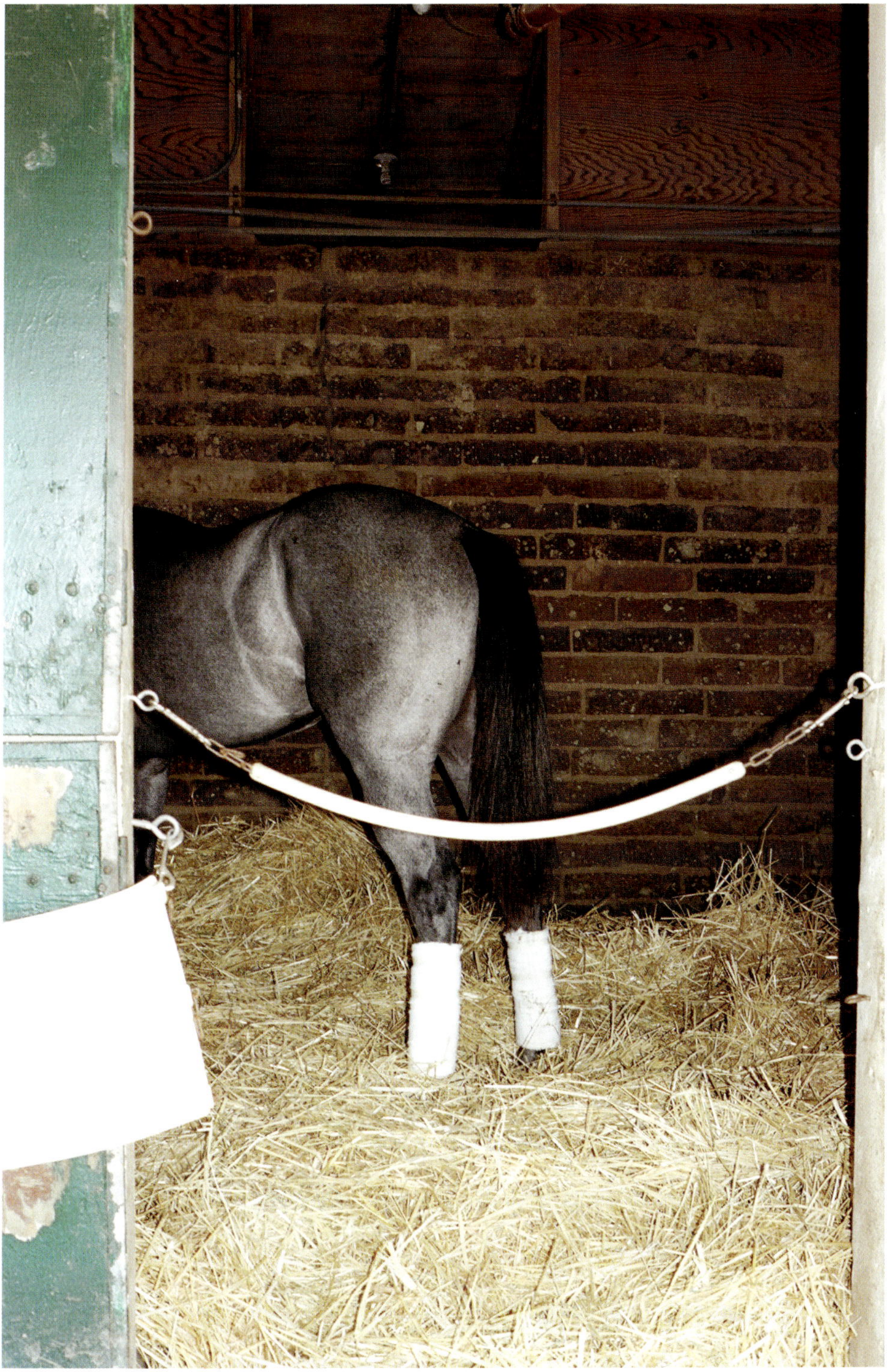

WESTRUX

11
CA

ALWAYS BELIEVE,
ALWAYS BELIEV
1

4
2
2

DELMAR
THOROUBRED CLUB

AMERICA

JEFF RUBY'S
STEAKHOUSES
2
2

DEL MAR
LEADING OWNERS
DEL MAR
LEADING TRAINERS
DEL
LEADING

RACE 7
8/17/14
5/8
1:01.45
FINISH
OYOTA
TVG

Love
Life
Get

MARGARET
Hospitality

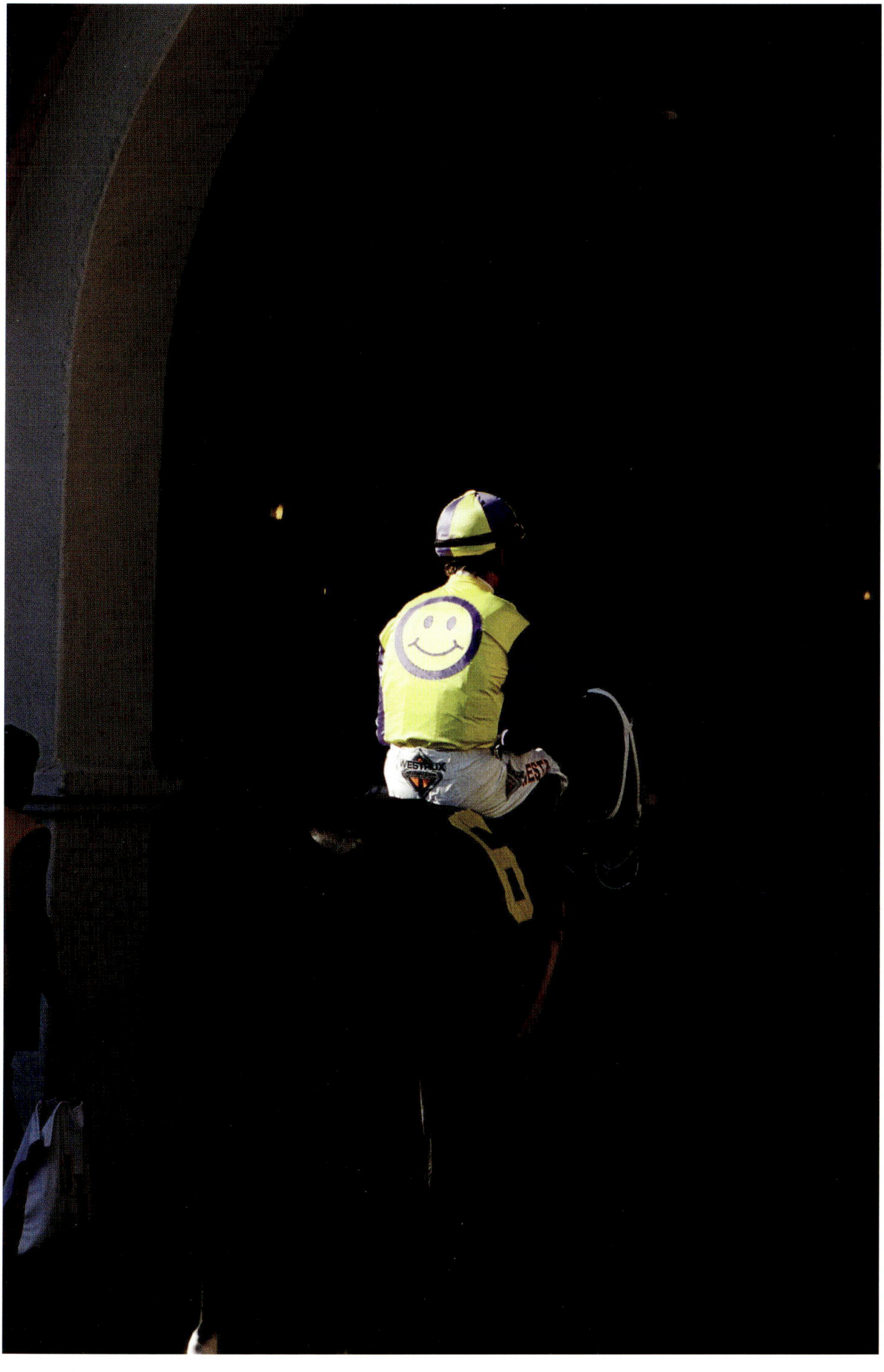

CHROME

GPA

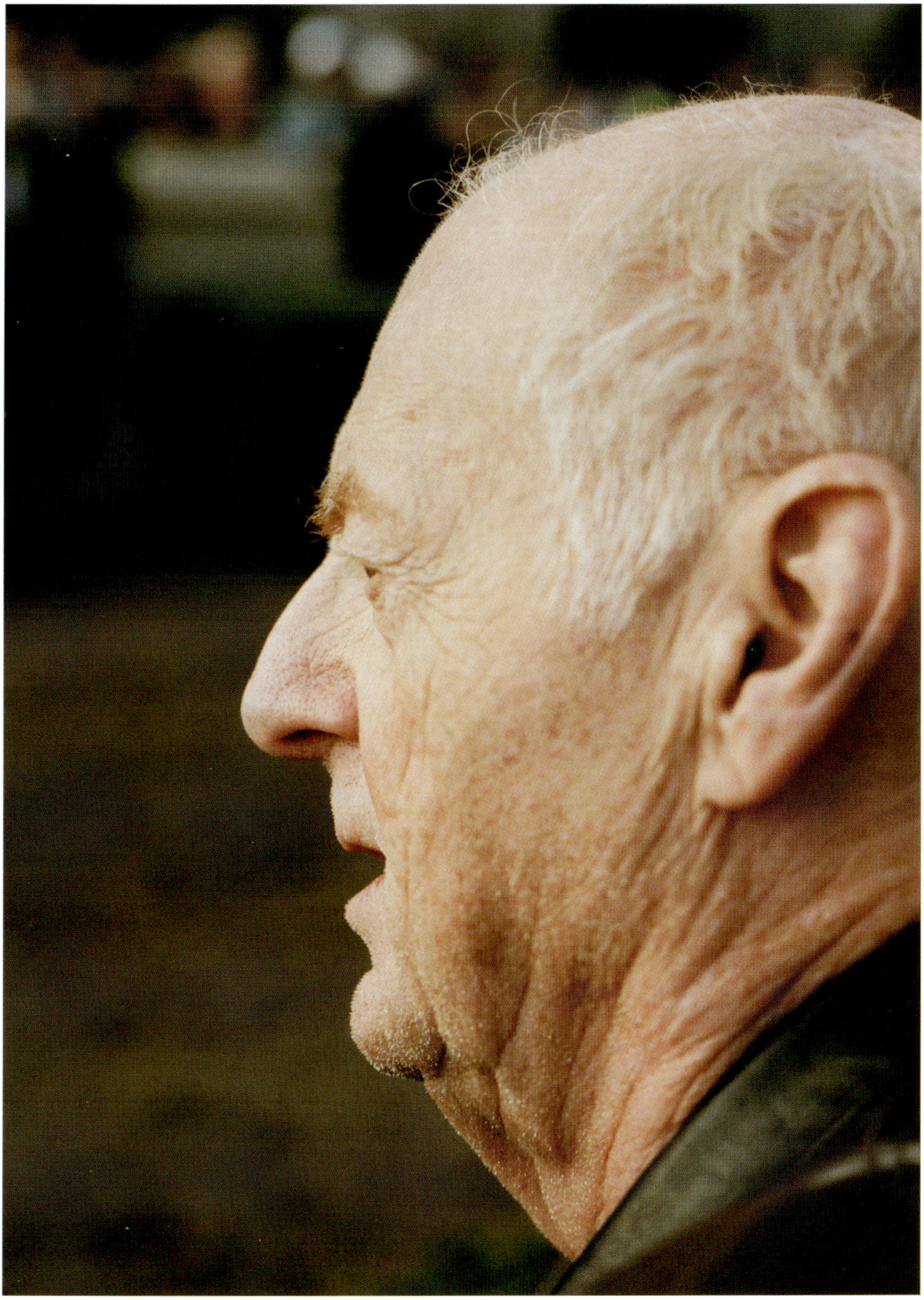

LA

DEL MAR
8 7 6 5 4 3 2 1

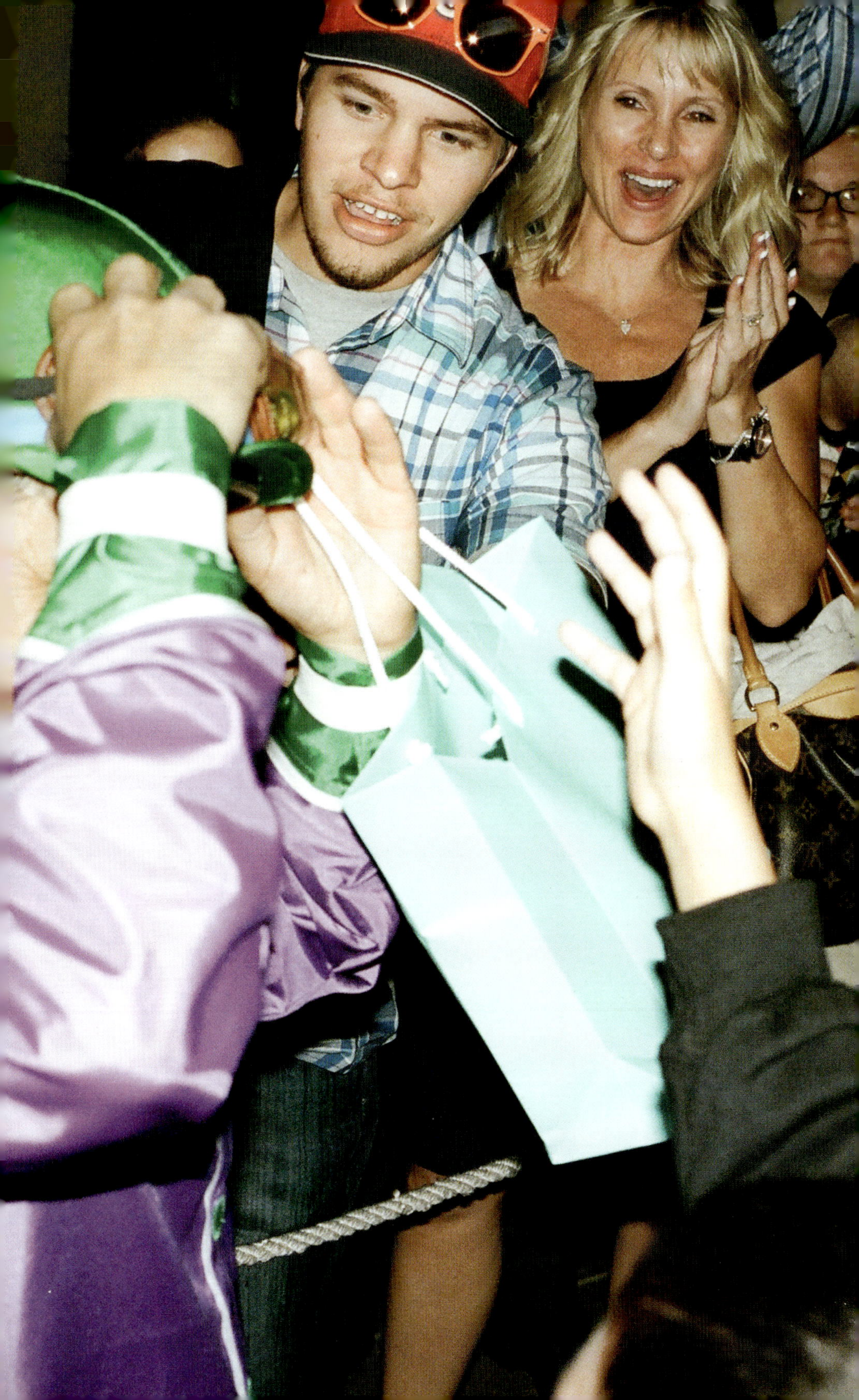

JOCKEYS
ONLY

HEARDSDALE

THRASHER
DEATH
DEADPOOL
19 91
MERC WITH A
MOUTH

COLD.

5
5

Albertsons
Sav-on

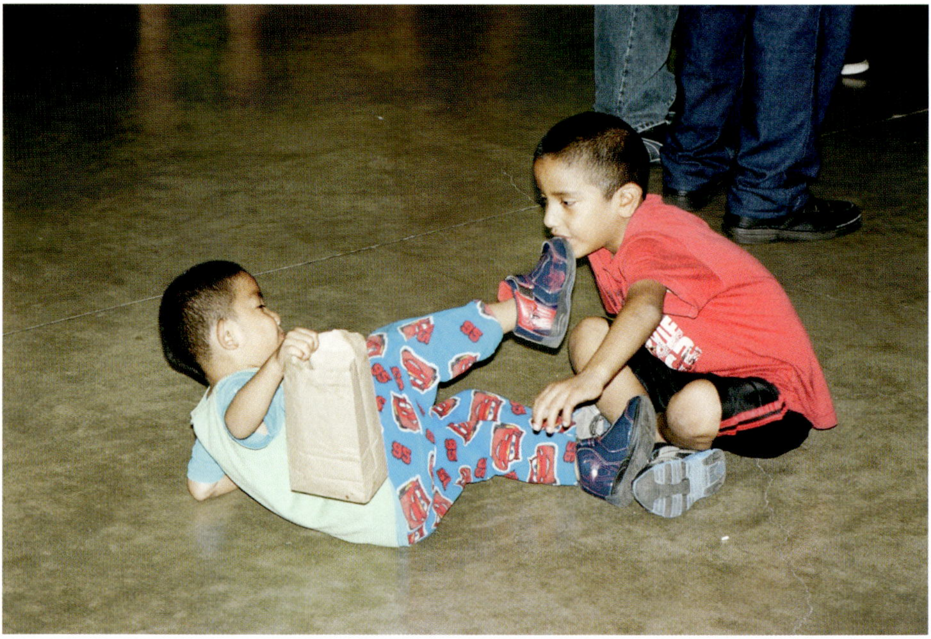

WESTRUX

at Del Mar
at Del Mar
Where the turf meets the

Race 3
DEL MAR
Race 2
DEL MAR
Race 2
DEL MAR
Race 2

Alaska
BNP PARIBAS
OPEN
FILA

M A R
DEL MAR
4
2

Breeders' Cup

All of us get Tired Feet
PLEASE BE POLITE
Let other people use massager
when you finish
Still only 25¢ - Quarters only
"THE ULTIMATE FOOT MASSAGE"
FOOTSIE WOOTSIE
RELAX · REJUVENATE · REVIVE
STILL ONLY
25¢
INSERT QUARTER
LEAVE SHOES ON
BE SEATED DO NOT STAND

All of us get Tired Feet
PLEASE BE POLITE
Let other people use massager when you finish
Still only 25¢ - Quarters only
"THE ULTIMATE FOOT MASSAGE"
FOOTSIE WOOTSIE
RELAX · REJUVENATE · REVIVE
STILL ONLY
25¢
INSERT QUARTER
LEAVE SHOES ON
BE SEATED DO NOT STAND

SF

SM

DE
FUEGO

CALIFORNIA CHROME

G
H

BETAMERICA

OCKEYS
ONLY

JEFF RUBY'S

CLUBHOUSE
LAMBERT

LL
NO
PARKING

KEENELAND
SEPTEMBER
YEARLING SALE
SEPTEMBER 8-21
PADDOCK TAVERN

Dove

3 3
CLOSED

AND AWAY THEY GO
Eric Chakeen

Special thanks to Jim and Tina Benedict,
Kelly and Jim Bialick, Cassie Goodman,
Eleanor Bialick, Chris Black, Steven Counts

Cover design by Dana Veraldi
Layout and design by Amardeep Singh
Published by Done to Death Projects
Printed in Korea through FCPG, Louisville, KY

Edition of 500

ISBN 978-1-61850-091-5